STEAM MOTIVE POWER CENTRE

No. 55: RETFORD

Including: The Motive Power Depots, Static ... *ne Main Lines*

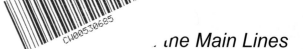

Copyright Book Law Publications 2009

ISBN 978-1-907094-47-7

INTRODUCTION PAGE

Described in the *Railway & Commercial Gazetteer* and by the Ordnance Survey as East Retford, the Nottinghamshire town of Retford had dropped the directional prefix at some unknown date after 1850, at least the railway companies serving the town did anyway. The first railway to reach the ancient market town was the Manchester, Sheffield & Lincolnshire in July 1849 on its eastwards drive from Sheffield to Gainsborough. During the following September the Great Northern arrived from the Doncaster direction but it was nearly three more years before the latter company completed its line from Peterborough giving access to London and later starting the passenger services on the East Coast Main Line (ECML). Each company set up their own engine sheds but shared the station, a situation that remaining until Grouping when it all became part of the LNER. Because the two railways met at Retford on the level and at virtually right angles to each other it was necessary to install a flat crossing where each main line crossed the others path. However, the arrangement was inconvenient for through passenger services between the two companies and reversing had to be resorted to during those first years. As early as 1857 the chord line from the Down side of the GN line was built to facilitate a run through from London to Manchester, the MS&LR tracks being gained at Whisker Hill junction. Over the next hundred or so years up to 1960, station improvements, track and signalling, besides new and larger engine sheds, were the only major alterations made to the layout at Retford - the 1960 layout was much the same as the 1860 layout, only the colours had changed.

Our photographic review of the railways around Retford covers the period when British Railways steam reached its zenith before its rapid decline into the diesel era. Keith Pirt had lineside passes for both the former Great Central route and the Great Northern route, besides umpteen other locations nation-wide. He made much use of them over the years from 1957 to 1965 and his colour photography records not just the motive power and the various trains but also the infrastructure on and around the main lines. To add further depth to his portfolio KRP ventured southwards along the ECML for a couple of miles to Gamston bank where some excellent smoke effects were presented by locomotives working hard and fast up the grade.

Of course Keith did not finish his railway photography when the diesels came - he carried on and in turn captured the best that the internal combustion engine could offer before electrification finally caught up with the ECML. However, the diesel pictures do not feature in this album - it is pure steam, all the way. The diesels will come later in their own album.

So, there we have Retford, a busy, interesting and somewhat unique railway centre which was pretty much unchanged from its early beginnings. It took well over a hundred years to get rid of the flat crossing at this place but when that event took place it was in a spectacular style and as we see the place today.

(Title Page) **The Gainsborough Model Railway Society special hauled by O4 No.63585 veers off the Lincoln-Sheffield line at Retford and heads for station's Down platform on Saturday 12th October 1963. Starting at midday from Lincoln (Central), the train picked up at Gainsborough (Lea Road), Retford and Worksop then took a circular tour to take in the freight lines of south Yorkshire. Being one of the original GCR 8K class 2-8-0s, dating from October 1911, the motive power was most appropriate to say the least. A fairly recent addition to the Retford shed stud, 36E had even gone to the trouble of cleaning the engine and painting the front bufferbeam. Its demise however was not long in coming and just before Christmas it was condemned. The October 1962 special run by the GMRS was hauled by the last of the Retford based J11s, No.64354, which took the annual outing over to the GN & LNWR Joint line from Nottingham to Market Harborough and later over the ECML from Peterborough to Grantham. *BLP - E34*

Printed and bound by The Amadeus Press, Cleckheaton, West Yorkshire

First published in the United Kingdom by Book Law Publications, 382 Carlton Hill, Nottingham, NG4 1JA

Off to work. In September 1958, J6 No.64178, with brake van in tow, waits at the signal to traverse the flat crossing and head off to one of the collieries located west of Retford. A recent arrival on the Retford allocation, ex Grantham, the 0-6-0 is quite clean considering its last visit to main works had taken place more than twelve months previously. Coming up to its forty-ninth birthday, No.64178 was somewhat younger than its driver according to Keith Pirt's notes. *BLP - E37*

3

History indeed. A Lincoln (Central) - Sheffield (Victoria) local passenger train takes the curve into Retford's Down platform in August 1959 behind D11 'Director' No.62669 YPRES. There is no sunshine, the engine is grubby and a bit rusty too but this picture is magical in recording the last vestiges of a once everyday occurrence which is impossible to enact anymore. Note the articulated coaching stock too. Darnall shed had the same problems as 52A and 34E and in fact most of the depots on BR at this time when it came to cleaners but the 4-4-0 had recently come out of storage and would soon return to that twilight zone, so why clean the dirt off which acts as a preserver - to a point. That was the logic behind the fact but when you have no cleaners available the logic seems doubly right and correct. Remarkably No.62669 survived another year in, and out, of traffic but eventually it passed on and was condemned on 12th August 1960 and immediately sent to Doncaster for scrapping. *BLP - E1255*

Not yet making its way home but instead running a trial to Barkston, N2 No.69535 clears Retford crossing at Ordsall on 30th October 1958 after overhaul at Doncaster works. The paint job and immaculate lining would be the last applied to the condensing tank before its withdrawal in September 1962. Shedded at King's Cross for most of its life, this engine was one of the last of its class to receive a major repair and treatment such as this. *BLP - E342*

Seen at Markham Moor in March 1962, York based Thompson A2/3 No.60516 HYCILLA has charge of a lightweight Sunday Only, Down 'Parly' including a six-wheel van on the back. *BLP- E360*

In the days before Southern Region Type 3 diesels started to run throughout on the Cliffe-Uddington bulk cement train on the ECML, this was the nearest you could get to such a working. V2 No.60889 has charge of a morning southbound train in June 1960 and is seen near Eaton Wood. The yellow hoppers seen here were based on the Airfix model or was it the other way round? Anyway, some of the 4-wheel vehicles must have been fairly new because they are still yellow, others in the formation have that coating of cement dust which was difficult to remove once a build-up started. Doncaster based No.60889 also had a build-up of dirt which would not be removed until its next visit to Darlington works, scheduled some six months hence, when separate cylinders would be fitted and outside steam pipes would change its profile somewhat. *BLP - E416*

7

With clear signals A4 No.60032 GANNET runs through Retford along the Up main in March 1961 with a non-stop, King's Cross bound, express. Retford North signal box was brought into operation in February 1875 as part of the layout improvement works carried out at Retford during that time. Saxby & Farmer supplied the new signals and the new box which replaced a previous, smaller cabin classified at the time on the GNR as a Second Class box - Retford South (known as Retford Tower before the 1870s improvements) had been a First Class establishment. In 1891 a new frame was installed to handle the increase in signals and points, as once again the railway system at Retford expanded into the one we see recorded here. Retford North signal box closed in March 1976 - one hundred and one years, and one month, after opening for business. *BLP - E446*

A well known figure to many of the local footplatemen, Keith Pirt managed to get these two on film whilst their train waits for signals at Ordsall in June 1959. One of the LNER wartime-built engines, O2 No.63972 still has the British Railways 'lion and wheel' crest and will continue to show it off until it goes to Doncaster for its last General overhaul in December 1960. During its short life the 2-8-0 served at five different sheds: Doncaster, Colwick, Langwith Junction, Mexborough and finally, from August 1951, Retford. All of those depots were concerned with the haulage of one commodity in particular - coal - and that appears to be the case today, although the second wagon contains something much different. *BLP - E448*

Having negotiated the Ollerton Road level crossing (now an overbridge), locally based J11 'Pom-Pom' No.64451 approaches the GC/GN flat crossing at Retford in September 1958 with a mixed freight from Worksop. The bridge in the left background offered a good vantage point of the junction at Whisker Hill where the loop from Retford station joined the Sheffield line to continue its east-west alignment. Note how straight the line is - from this point it remained so for nearly five miles towards Worksop. Beyond the road crossing there were passing loops and sidings on both Up and Down sides of the line, the level crossing itself forming a bottle-neck prior to the ECML rail crossing also creating a similar problem. This 0-6-0 had been a resident of Thrumpton shed since transferring from Frodingham in October 1947. It was to be its last shed and 1958 would prove to be its final full year of operation - in December 1959 it attended Gorton works for a 'General' but was condemned and cut up instead. Its place was taken by an O4. *BLP - E48*

The short-lived *ANGLO SCOTTISH CAR CARRIER* was born at the end of the steam age and just managed to last long enough to be diesel hauled before it too was withdrawn. Here south of Retford, A3 No.60044 MELTON speeds the Up train beneath Eaton Wood bridge on a glorious summer afternoon in June 1963. Note that the train consists of six of the double-deck 'covered wagons' which could accommodate up to seven saloon cars, an increase of two over the original single deck CCTs in use since 1955. The other five vehicles make up the passenger accommodation. Introduced in 1961 for the *CAR-SLEEPER LIMITED* overnight services between King's Cross and Perth, the new Eastern Region Car Transporter (to give it the title painted on the bodyside) weighed in at 32 tons unladen but could carry a load of 12½ tons. So successful was the Anglo-Scottish overnight service that a daytime working between Holloway and Edinburgh had been introduced in 1960 and these vehicles, as can be seen, became regulars on that too. Equipped with both automatic vacuum brake and Westinghouse air brake, the carriages were equipped to work abroad - how useful that would have been now. Outside contractors Newton Chambers Ltd. of Sheffield, supplied fourteen of the new double-deck carriages to BR which, because of their apparent bulk, looked impressive when in train formations such as this. Although the ASCC was in effect a 'named train' it did not always carry a headboard, especially when diesel hauled. The Pacific would have taken over this train at Newcastle (Central) and Gateshead shed were notorious for losing train headboards and that, perhaps, was the reason for the lack of one adorning the smokebox here. However, with King's Cross shed about to close the missing headboard may well have been a.w.o.l. already, who knows?. MELTON was condemned on 16th of the month and this could have been its last Up working. Its final Down working, although not in steam, was to Doncaster Plant works where it was cut up in November. *BLP - E456*

For all the bad publicity generated against Edward Thompson and his so-called 'meddling' with Gresley's Pacifics, his meddling of the Robinson O4 class to create what was envisaged, by him, as the standard LNER 2-8-0 freight locomotive, turned out this nicely proportioned Class O1 engine. These 2-8-0s were useful machines which came a little too late to be perhaps fully appreciated by all and sundry. Certainly the London Midland Region did not rate them and when Annesley engine shed came under LMR control in 1962 all the Thompson O1s were condemned en masse (even those which had recently returned from major overhauls at Gorton) and, as if to rub salt into the wounds, most of them were then sent to the former LMS locomotive workshops at either Crewe or Derby for scrapping. Events such as that made us realise at the time that steam had no further use on British Railways and their rapid demise was quickly forthcoming. No.63650, here at Retford in May 1961, was originally a Class O4/3 engine, rebuilt to O1 standard in May 1945 as LNER No.6545. The engine had recently returned to traffic from overhaul at Gorton during the previous February and March and on this day was a visitor from Staveley. Although finishing work when allocated to Langwith Junction shed in June 1965, it was later sold to a scrap metal merchant in Norfolk. *BLP - E481*

With the crew taking an interest in KRP, York based Thompson A2/3 No.60518 TEHRAN nears Retford for a station stop with a Down express in August 1961. Only six months out from a 'General' the Pacific is not looking its best, especially around the lower edge of the smokebox door. Only sixteen years old at the time of its withdrawal, it would be interesting to know just how long this engine (and perhaps hundreds of others) would have lasted if dieselisation had not been a priority for British Railways. Note the sludge tender tucked away at the end of the siding. *BLP - E483*

Gingerly approaching the flat crossing tender first from the west, Gresley O2 No.63937, with a Great Northern type cab, makes its way towards Thrumpton engine shed with said tender virtually empty. On this May in 1961 the 2-8-0 and appears to be in good external condition even though the last visit to Doncaster Plant had taken place some seven months previously. The straight sided, 4200 gallon, Group Standard tender (No.T5620 and ex K3 class) was coupled to the engine at that October 1960 'General' and was the engines sixth tender since it came into traffic at the end of 1923; the other five had been GNR tenders of varying types. The coupling of O2 class engines fitted with GN cabs but coupled to LNER GS tenders was not quite unique but it was rare. Somewhere else in this album I have mentioned the AWS warning system battery box being fitted beneath the cab, alongside the steps. Here we see the left-handed version as applied by Doncaster - was this the only place to fit the box? Note the new and recently laid flat-bottomed rail now furnishing this east-west route. It was to be another two years or so before work on the dive-under would start here in earnest and the flat crossing, with all its inherent dangers would become history. However, that was some time off and steam at Retford still had plenty of work to do before it too became history. *BLP - E487*

14

Shortly after passing through Retford, and now kicking up a fair amount of smoke, Dairycoates based K3 No.61899 leads the late running 2.55 p.m. fish train from Hull's Outward Yard to King's Cross Goods up the gradient of Gamston bank near Eaton Wood in August 1961. In 1952, for instance, the port of Hull sent out twelve fish trains every day except Saturdays when only ten were run but on Mondays fourteen were sent out, all between midday and 9.00 p.m. This formation was typical of the number of vehicles (25 to 30) run in most of the trains but changing trends, both in the appetite of the population and the method of transport meant that the fish trains run by British Railways would not have much longer to run and their demise virtually coincided with the end of steam on BR. In 1964 the total number of fish trains run on BR was twenty-five daily and that was to be cut before the end of the year when some of those originating from the west coast port at Fleetwood were withdrawn. Also in 1964 a new road haulage company Hull Fish Transport Ltd., was formed by Hull fish merchants. BR meanwhile proposed to fish merchants that fish traffic should be concentrated into block loads to central distribution points with road transport then taking over for local distribution. By its very nature fish does not take well to too much handling so the BR idea did not go down well with the industry - it was no wonder that road won the day. By the end of 1964 the Hull fish traffic on BR was down to one train a day, an evening service to King's Cross. BR, apparently, lost half a million pounds revenue from the loss of the Hull workings alone. The end is almost upon this Gresley 2-6-0 too but another year of working jobs like this would see it visit London a few more times before its December 1962 withdrawal. One of the Armstrong Whitworth built members of the class, No.61899 came into traffic during March 1931 and was allocated to various sheds in what became the North Eastern Region of BR throughout its life. Despite this photograph being late in the life of the class, with certain engines already condemned and scrapped, this particular engine went into Doncaster Plant works during December 1961 and emerged in the following February having had a General overhaul with a change of boiler and a fresh coat of black paint, albeit unlined. *BLP - E51*

Another variant of the Robinson 2-8-0 O4 class at Retford in April 1959 was No.63688, one of the ninety-nine Part 8 engines. Recently ex works, this 2-8-0 is resting on the shed yard at Thrumpton under a glorious Sunday afternoon sky. Coaled up (with some nice pieces too), watered and turned ready for its Monday morning duty, the engine will no doubt be heading a coal train. The Part 8 O4s were the last former Great Central locomotives working on BR and they were amongst the last of Eastern Region steam when the last of the class were condemned in April 1966 - a fitting tribute to a superb design which had its origins in pre-WW1 days. This particular locomotive was built by private contractors in February 1918 for the Ministry of Munitions but was then stored until the LNER purchased it from the Government in 1924. It came to Retford in December 1943 as LNER No.6343 and resided until the shed closed in June 1965. During October 1956 it was rebuilt to Part 8 standard. Prior to this photograph being taken it had just returned from a Heavy Intermediate overhaul at Gorton which finished 24th March. Prior to its 26th September 1965 withdrawal, it would visit Gorton twice more, in 1962 for a boiler change and General overhaul, and then in March 1963 for repairs to minor collision damage. During the few months before its demise, it was working from Doncaster shed, its home before its wartime transfer to Retford. *BLP - E49*

Grubby but nonetheless still graceful, A3 No.60107 ROYAL LANCER heads an Up express, made up entirely of BR Mk1 coaches by now, through the short cutting at Ordsall in May 1963. It is often forgotten in this age of motorways and by-passes that the old A1 trunk road (Great North Road) ran through the centre of Retford until recent times and the road bridge carrying the A1 over the railway can just be made out behind the tree with the signal beneath. Naturally the railway builders of the 19th Century, or to be more precise the builders of the Great Northern Railway, followed the course of the GN Rd (no coincidence there) for much of the time between London and Doncaster whereas now the trunk road has progressed into motorway standard dual-carriageway for much of its length and runs parallel though usually some distance from the ECML. With a slight dig at the motoring lobby, the roads do seem to attract a lot of public money compared to the railways and in an effort to lessen the shock of the costs involved the road planners have built their pristine replacement roadways over a period of time, in short to medium length stretches (5 to 20 miles for instance) - stealth like. Now if someone came up with a plan to replace the present ECML with a completely new railway (TGV-like) which would link Edinburgh to London in just two hours or less perhaps, and which could be completed in four years or so at a cost of £!!! billion, oh and be environmentally friendly, then that same person would be castigated by many, including the media and certain political groups, as being a 'nutter' or christened with some such derogatory title. However, the ECML still works. It even has capacity for more traffic though speeds could not be raised much more. So, enjoy this glimpse of an A3 sauntering along at a leisurely 65 m.p.h. or so, and remember how slow and perhaps much better life used to be not so long ago. *BLP - E511*

17

I wonder if Gateshead motive power depot ever communicated with their headquarters and informed them that 52A had a problem '... we can't get any cleaners...' Besides the filth problem, the bufferbeam of V2 No.60979 appears to be as rusty as the sides of the rails and it isn't a colour imperfection with the original film either. Seen running through the sweeping curve at the south end of Retford station, the 2-6-2 is heading a Newcastle express in August 1961. The engine had long since used up all its overhaul places and was reliant now on Gateshead shed keeping it going. They managed it for another year but gave up on 1st October 1962 and condemned the big engine - it was just eighteen years old. On the last day of January 1963 it entered its place of birth at Darlington having attained nineteen years and was then dismantled. *BLP - E517*

Another non-stop Up express passes the signal box at Retford North in June 1960, this with A3 No.60055 WOOLWINDER at its head. Besides the more well known and famous flat crossing at the south end of the station, Retford could boast another flat crossing within its precincts. Just to the left of the signal box the access roads to the former Great Northern engine shed, and the line from the station's west side Down platform to the Down main have to cross the Retford-Sheffield loop or chord line. The siting of the signal box gives excellent all round vision but if the 'bobby' got it wrong the box itself might become involved in any collision. However, the 10 m.p.h. speed restriction on the Sheffield line minimises both collision and major damage. A similar speed restriction existed for the shed line too. Stand by for the Pacific and its train to rattle over the points to the right of the cameraman - what an unforgettable sound! *BLP - E540* 19

With four milk churns full of water, B1 No.61231 sets out from Thrumpton with supplies for the various crossing keepers and signal boxes along the former GCR (Manchester, Sheffield & Lincolnshire Railway) route east of Retford - Clarborough being one such location. Scenes such as this were common in rural areas of the country where signal boxes were somewhat isolated from the rest of civilisation and winter supplies became difficult after sub zero temperatures. Coal too would be supplied for the stove and fireplaces - all totally dependant on the railway. Generations of signalmen would testify that you never did quite get used to the isolation of some boxes on a stormy winter night when the only company was the pot bellied stove, its ever present boiling kettle and the bell signals from adjacent similarly situated boxes. The crossing keepers though had their cottages which because of the permanence and the nature of the job kept them restricted to the place. At least the signal bobbies could go home at the change of shift. The footbridge spanning both the east-west main line and the engine shed yard can be seen in the background whilst the north wall of the engine shed casts a shadow over the Down line and its adjacent loop. Besides coal mining, evidence of other local industry can be seen in the shape of the malt houses to the right of the picture. The date is sometime in February 1959. *BLP - E551*

What's this then? Has the station buffet run out milk or something much worse, water? Thompson B1 No.61231 heads tender first for Retford station after its water duties out in the country. This aspect of the former GC line, looking westwards, affords a good view of the approach to the ECML crossing and the signal box which controlled traffic over it - Retford South. This particular signal box dates from December 1874 and replaced another structure known as Retford Tower which was classified by the Great Northern Railway as a First Class signal box. It would be interesting to know what the 'Tower' looked like and was it, for instance, anything like the one at Honington Junction which had two enormous signal posts above the box itself. Because Retford South box controlled two very important main lines converging on the same level, what kind of signals existed before the 1874 alterations?. *BLP - E750*

Boasting just two through roads, the former Great Central engine shed at Thrumpton was rather cramped for its resident allocation so the yard to the east and south of the place sufficed to 'house' the residents at weekends when, by mid afternoon on Saturday everyone was at home. Sunday was a good time to visit as a 'spotter' but photography became somewhat restricted so that only engines on the outer roads of the gathering could be 'snapped'. O2 class No.63970 has managed to reserve a place on the west end of No.1 shed road, albeit out in the open but the weather is fine and sunny so what the heck. The shed here was reroofed by BR shortly after Nationalisation and in this March 1959 view the ravages of a few short years have already taken a toll on the 'new' brickwork. Having been standing for one hundred and ten years, the place did not have much longer to resist the smoke and pollution because as part of the dive-under scheme this shed was to be demolished to make way for the realignment of the east-west main line. The 2-8-0 was one of the wartime 1942 batch which ended up at Retford in August 1951. Compared with most, No.63970 was an early casualty being withdrawn in May 1960, not quite eighteen years old. Perhaps the shock of its condemnation was to soften us up for the later withdrawals which accounted for engines seven years or less of age being condemned because they were in the wrong depot at the wrong time! *BLP - E572*

22

Ex works Thompson B1 No.61208 departs from Retford along the GC route with an eastbound train on a chilly, late October day in 1958. In the distance can be seen the signal box controlling the level crossing which crossed the main line and the Thrumpton engine shed yard too. The shed itself can be discerned as the dark shape to the left of the box. When work on the new diveunder was begun in 1963, the new railway was fitted into the vacant space immediately to the right of the loop line here, the elegant signal gantry being a casualty of the new alignment. The 4-6-0 was one of Retford's own and had just completed a 'General' at Doncaster on the 10th of the month. The engine had been at Retford since new in July 1947 and would remain 'on the books' until June 1965 when the able remnants of 36E (only the former Great Northern shed was still operational up to then, the ex GC shed having been closed in January and then being demolished) were sent to the few surviving depots still under Eastern Region control. No.61208 went to Doncaster but did little work from there and it was condemned in September. *BLP - E619*

23

It is a nice warm June evening in 1962 and local O4 No.63764 makes its way out of the sidings at the north of the station. Not too much effort is required to make up its train and the crew do not appear to be exerting much anyway. To sit and watch a big 2-8-0 shunt stock at a leisurely pace on a pleasant summer evening, whilst the occasional express sprints by to some far off destination, was heaven to many. Another of the Government's war surplus engines, this one was stored for just over ten years before the LNER bought it in May 1928 but it was a bargain even then having hardly turned a wheel from new. As can be seen it remained a Part 3 variant of the class throughout its civilian railway career. The last vestiges of clean black paint are just about to disappear from its boiler after its recent 'General' at Gorton - its last repair incidentally. A newcomer to Retford shed in November 1960, the 2-8-0 transferred to Doncaster in March 1963 but remained in traffic until the end of February 1966 when its withdrawal finally took place. *BLP - E629*

Just a little later during that June 1962 evening, a northbound express is restarted from its Retford stop by A4 No.60010 DOMINION OF CANADA. This views offers another aspect of Retford North signal box, with the station Down island platform behind, and showing the engine shed and platform lines joining the Down main. *BLP - E632*

25

Earlier that evening, at the south end of the station (with the lineside pass paying dividends), an immaculate A4 No.60034 LORD FARINGDON was captured on film heading back to Doncaster after a trial run to Barkston triangle. The Pacific's tender is running across the line linking the westbound GC route with the Retford station No.3 west side (Down) platform. Just in the frame on the right is the Down goods loop. No.60034 had just completed its last General overhaul, appropriately at Doncaster, and would soon work south to its home shed at King's Cross; that particular journey saw it work a goods train all the way to London. The 'General' stood the engine in good stead for another life after ECML workings when Top Shed closed in June 1963. Like most of the remaining Pacifics at 34A, this one was transferred to New England where most went into storage. During the following October No.60034 was chosen to go to St Margarets and, after six months there, to Aberdeen Ferryhill for a two year stint on the Aberdeen-Glasgow expresses. During its time at Aberdeen it received a rather long-winded three and a half months Heavy Intermediate overhaul at Darlington works in early 1965. However, the major repair kept the Pacific going until the end of steam workings on the 3-hour expresses. It travelled one last time back to England but only as far as North Blyth where scrap merchant Hughes, Bolckow cut it up during the winter of 1966. Note the stuck-open casing hatch cover revealing the new asbestos lagging on the boiler. *BLP - E635*

Those 'Parly' trains got shorter by the month. This is A3 No.60046 DIAMOND JUBILEE approaching Retford crossing in June 1962 with just two coaches in tow. *BLP - E641*

Gresley A4 No.60014 SILVER LINK rolls to a halt at Retford with an Up stopping train from Leeds (Central) to King's Cross in June 1962. Although the nameplate of the Pacific is nicely cleaned, the bodywork is showing signs of neglect as this was to be the A4's last summer of operation. The engine had just come out of Doncaster 'Plant' after a Casual Light repair (8th to 22nd June) but a fresh coat of paint or even a clean was obviously not 'on the cards' for what proved to be its last visit to works for maintenance. Withdrawn on 29th December, it was taken into Doncaster for cutting up on 16th January 1963, twenty-eight years after it had emerged from that place as LNER No.2509 to take up its rightful position in railway history. Its former exploits in dragging the LNER to the forefront of streamlined passenger travel had conveniently been forgotten by the end of 1962 when all thoughts were on the dieselisation of the East Coast main line. Such is progress. *BLP - E680*

SILVER LINK stands just proud of the curving platform face awaiting the whistle from the guard. The signal is pegged ready and the Down side of the station is quiet for the moment. The tracks leading off to the left serve the westernmost platform (No.3) of the station and a goods loop. Access to the Sheffield line was possible from the platform line but not from the goods line, the latter being for northbound ECML freight trains only. Locomotive access to the former Great Northern engine shed was possible from either of these lines. Retford North signal box is visible at the far end of the Down platform, and bells will soon be heard inside signifying more main line action. A pedestrian subway passed beneath this junction exactly below where the photographer is standing; the footpath led to Ollerton Road situated west of the engine shed. *BLP - E640*

29

June 1963 on the ECML. Daises try to take over the lineside foliage but who is complaining. The sky is clear, shirt sleeves were the order for the day and steam still works some of the traffic on the line. This is O4/1 No.63607 rolling downgrade past the crossing keeper's house at Eaton Wood with a train of petroleum tanks, complete with two barrier wagons just in case. The dirty 2-8-0 was one of Retford's own complement which had transferred from Colwick during the previous December - the dirt came with it and never was wiped off. One of the original Great Central engines inherited by the LNER, No.63607 was put to work in January 1912 and spent much of its life up to the end of the LNER at Mexborough shed. Colwick shed got the engine back in June 1965 but it was condemned during the following September and immediately sold for scrap. Its last recorded heavy overhaul took place during the summer of 1958, Gorton releasing the engine to traffic on 9th August. It that was the case then this remarkable engine worked for seven years without any further heavy maintenance other than what the home depots could provide. *BLP - E673*

SILVER LINK in balmier days in charge of the southbound set of *THE ELIZABETHAN* in August 1961. *BLP - E36*

The Retford breakdown crane and its accompanying vans sets off along the Up main line at Ordsall behind grubby B1 No.61302 in October 1962. The express headlamps indicate the train is proceeding to an incident somewhere to the south. Note the vivid red livery of the vans - a GNR bogie coach and a modified Gresley Brake - whilst the steam crane wears a sombre black livery. The positioning of an open wagon at the rear of the formation was unusual. The B1 was from New England (hence the external appearance) and must have been borrowed by 36E for this particular job but it would soon be off to Doncaster for a General overhaul which would take it through to April 1966 when, as a resident of Colwick shed, it was withdrawn by the London Midland Region. *BLP- 708*

Having just gained the Worksop line at Whisker Hill junction, beneath the bridge, Doncaster based B1 No.61135 recovers from its Retford station stop and continues it journey to Sheffield with this afternoon train from Cleethorpes in April 1963. For the next four miles or so of the westbound working, the line is dead straight until Manton Wood where the first of numerous collieries start to appear along the route. Until October 1959, this 4-6-0 worked on the former Great Eastern lines of the Eastern Region and would rarely, if ever, have worked to Retford during that time. However, its time now was at a premium because once the summer timetable was abandoned, the B1 would be condemned and taken into the works at Doncaster for scrapping. *BLP - E800*

The fastest of them all! Looking the part, A4 No.60022 MALLARD heads the northbound *FLYING SCOTSMAN* over the bridge spanning a tranquil Idle in July 1960. *BLP - E835*

One of the most famous non-railway names known to the post-war enthusiast was that of the Northern Rubber Co. at Retford. The company organised an annual outing to Blackpool which was hauled throughout by one of the various well known LNER Pacifics. Carrying the headboard *NORTHERN RUBBER SPECIAL*, the excursion usually gave Lancashire based railway enthusiasts the chance to see one of the ECML engines, always turned out immaculately, working over routes where they did not normally run. Behind the annual event was one Alan Pegler who then went on to become famous himself as owner and operator of FLYING SCOTSMAN. The 1960 event saw MALLARD take twelve coaches, with 320 occupants, to Blackpool on Saturday September 30th but the dozen vehicles consisted more than just passenger coaches. Within the formation were two kitchen cars and a buffet car whilst bringing up the rear was observation car M 280 which had just been released from its summer duties on the Inverness-Kyle of Lochalsh line. At Blackpool, for the return journey, which departed at midnight, two sleeping cars replaced the observation car to bring the number of carriages up to thirteen but the weight of the train itself was considerably enhanced to 490 tons. In order to counteract the extra load, No.60022 had the preserved Midland compound No.1000 doubleheading from Blackpool (North). It would have been a treat to have seen the 4-4-0 piloting the Pacific but alas the whole journey took place in darkness so the opportunity was never there. In this February 1959 view the NR Co. factory itself can be seen on the left as Thompson B1 No.61056 heads special working No.554 through Thrumpton on a cold but nevertheless glorious morning. Note that the 4-6-0 is carrying yellow and green flags over the front bufferbeam signifying that the special was carrying Norwich City football club (The Canaries) supporters to a game at Sheffield. Norwich shed have done an excellent job with the engine's appearance but I should imagine that the passenger accommodation could not match that of the NRC's annual outings. I have no idea which of the Sheffield clubs were playing nor the result of the match, which is a pity . *BLP - E838*

Weak November sun, nice steamy exhaust, its that 'Streak' again. No.60022 hurries through Ordsall with a southbound express in 1960. BLP - E852

In this November 1960 picture of B1 No.61392, passing through Ordsall with a heavy south bound mixed freight, the cylinders look larger than normal. However, the dirt encrusting the front face of them is emphasised by the direct sunlight. The Grantham based 4-6-0 appears decidedly filthy, which was unusual for 34F, but was between overhauls, with its last one being carried out in January 1958 whilst its next one did not take place until September 1962! With all the Pacifics allocated to Grantham shed, it would seem that the mixed traffic locomotives did not rate too highly in the cleaning order. As part of the scheme to equip all the Eastern Region locomotives with AWS, No.61392 had recently attended Doncaster works for a Non-Classified repair to have the parts fitted - evidence of that visit can be seen beneath the front buffer beam where the electrical circuitry and magnetic receiver hid behind the front coupling guard. *BLP - E875* 37

It is February 1959 and the fleeting glimpse of the firebox glow would have been missed by the photographer as he concentrated in getting this nice rear three-quarter view of A3 No.60062 MINORU gracefully pulling away from Retford with a northbound train in glorious sunshine. It is a Sunday afternoon and the rails leading off to the left are those to Worksop and Sheffield which appear to have been little used during the previous twenty-four hours, at least in the Down direction. *BLP - E696*

The Peppercorn K1 was a useful mixed traffic engine able to put itself into any situation but by 1960 most of the work carried out by the class, wherever they were shedded, was goods haulage. Retford shed had nine of them by June 1962, all ex March, which had trickled across from the Fens since the previous September. Four of them left for Doncaster in November 1962, No.62051 amongst them but it only arrived in May 1962. Looking respectfully clean for the period, the 2-6-0 stands outside the east end of Thrumpton shed in August 1962 between a pair of Gresley O2. For the record, the other K1 allocated to Retford were Nos.62015 9/61–11/62; 62019 9/61–7/64 withdrawal; 62037 10/61–11/62; 62039 4/62–12/63 withdrawal; 62040 10/61–11/62; 62054 10/61–12/64 withdrawal; 62067 5/62–1/65; 62070 6/6/2–1/65 withdrawal. For the modeller this picture contains plenty of interesting hues to the grey and black which predominate the colour. The ground is far from level with heaps of ash and clinker virtually everywhere with some of the track more or less hidden from this angle. The K1 has been cleaned to so extent above the running plate but below, including the cylinders, the sheen of the oily grime tells another story. *BLP - E895*

39

It is May 1960 and although the main line diesels are starting to build-up their numbers, the coal train operation around this part of the Eastern Region is still firmly in the hands of steam. Gresley Class O2/3 No.63949, one of the numerous Retford based 2-8-0s, is skirting platform No.1 as it rounds the curve from the ECML onto the Lincoln line with a coal train. Note the mixture of steel and wooden bodied wagons, new and old, battered and stained - typical fare for a mineral train. This view also affords us a look at the flat crossing of the ECML and Sheffield-Lincoln routes which was soon to be eliminated by an east-west 'diveunder' because of an expected increase in freight (coal) traffic over the east-west line. But that was still some time off and for the time being the signalmen controlling this 'disaster waiting to happen' just got on with their job and kept the traffic flowing safely and to time. The amount of sky left in this view might be considered excessive by some readers but a careful perusal will reveal a lot of wires passing from one side to the other between two or more hidden poles. Because of their nature, telephone and telegraph wires are one of those obvious yet rarely 'seen' bits of infrastructure which are nearly always neglected by railway modellers. Admitted, it would be a brave man who would tackle the amount of aerial wiring required to emulate this junction but even where less 'busy' sections of air space are modelled, the wires and their supporting post and columns are rarely featured - perhaps the wires really are there but are so thin as to be almost invisible. *BLP - E726*

O4 class No.63824 approaches the flat crossing from the west with a mixed freight train in October 1962. The freight traffic on the former GC route did not offer too much variety in the way of locomotive classes with J11 0-6-0, O1, O2, O4, and WD 2-8-0s being the usual suspects but O4 class did show up in all seven of their different variants. No.63824 had been rebuilt to a Part 7 engine in May 1943, one of forty-one to receive a shortened barrel O2 boiler and firebox whilst retaining the original GC cab and new GC style smokebox. By now it was a Retford engine having transferred from Frodingham in January 1960. Its next move was to Doncaster Plant works in July 1963 for cutting up after it June 1963 withdrawal. *BLP - E731*

How about this for a bulled-up K3? No.61934 has in fact just finished a 'General' at Doncaster and is running-in during early June 1960 under the auspices of the works testing regime - note the large front lamp on the centre iron. The engine is near Askham tunnel, en route to Barkston triangle where the 2-6-0 will turn for the run back to Doncaster The Tweedmouth based engine is turned out as though it is about to haul a train for royalty but this is in fact the condition that Doncaster works sent out its charges after major overhauls. Even the smokebox door securing handles are set tidily at a quarter past six. After twenty-seven years working from former North Eastern sheds, the K3 came south to Ardsley in September 1961 to work out its final year. Its next visit to Doncaster Plant in November 1962 saw it come out in little pieces inside wagons bound for the steel furnaces of Scunthorpe. *BLP - E744*

It has not been recorded how many times A4 No.60014 hauled *THE ELIZABETHAN* but it was undoubtedly a favourite Top Shed engine for the working. Here in August 1961, and turned out immaculately as usual, SILVER LINK is whisking the Down Edinburgh express past Eaton Wood under threatening skies. *BLP - E735*

The light cast by the morning sun is soft, warm and most welcome after the long hours of darkness. O2 No.63924 is bathed in the glow of an October 1963 morning as it moves off shed at Thrumpton for its day of toil, working coal trains from the collieries situated to the west of Retford. One of the Great Northern built members of the class, the original cab was replaced with this side window cab in 1939 and No.63924 became one of the last operational O2s. The locomotive arrived at Retford in September 1952 from Mexborough and stayed to the end. Within a couple of weeks of this moment in time being captured for ever, the 2-8-0 will have been condemned and sent to Doncaster for scrapping. As Thrumpton engine shed gradually got rid of its Gresley O2 engines, they were replaced by an equal number of WD Austerity 2-8-0s and a rather grotty unkempt member of that class, seen in the right background contrasts nicely with the white painted residential property on the left. Note the graffiti adorning the O2. *BLP - E772*

Starting away from Thrumpton yard on a sunny yet cold October day in 1962 (the winter to remember was just around the corner), local O2 class No.63975 heads east with a lightly loaded permanent way train The ex GCR bracket signal gives prior warning of the approaching junction for westbound passenger trains which called at the station; through freight traffic crossed the junction unheeded going due west and controlled by the left of the two signals. The former Great Central Railway engine shed stood behind the road bridge (the old A1) to the left, or at least its yard did, the shed itself, with engines simmering outside, can just be made out beneath the bridge. On this side of the bridge was a parachute water tank where eastbound engines could stop to replenish their tanks clear of the ECML crossing. The 2-8-0 was ex works during the previous July and some of the shine is still visible - in just twelve months time it will be condemned and cut up at Doncaster. *BLP - E952* 45

Just a couple of miles south of Retford at Gamston, where the ECML sweeps round from the south-east, is Gamston signal box where a nice view of the main line can be achieved. Double chimney A3 No.60073 ST GATIEN is captured heading a Down Newcastle express in June 1960. The tiny amount of exhaust being generated by the Pacific cannot reveal the reason why the class had to be fitted with the smoke deflectors. *BLP - E490*

Another A3 with a northbound express wheels round the curve as it descends Gamston bank and past the isolated signal box in August 1961. This is No.60105 VICTOR WILD which has both double chimney and smoke deflectors. With only a hint of an exhaust, it is impossible to see the effect of the deflectors. Compare the view with that opposite showing No.60073. The engine would have joined the train at Grantham, its home shed, where the cleaning problem has now started to affect the Pacifics. However, the picture is still good enough to include and brings back bucket loads of nostalgia. *BLP - E880*

Still on Gamston bank in August 1961, we see A3 No.60039 SANDWICH ascending the grade hauling an Up express with apparent ease.
48 Looking rather clean and tasty, the engine is performing a task which it had done literally thousands of times through its lifetime. *BLP - E85*

V2s, no matter what condition they were in, did not visit the Thrumpton shed too often so it is nice to have this record of No.60858's visit in August 1962. The New England based 2-6-2 has green livery beneath that coating of grime but it is debatable if it was ever seen again before the engine went for scrap in January 1964. Note the double chimney, fitted at its October 1961 and final General overhaul. When King's Cross shed closed in June 1963, the bulk of its Pacific allocation were sent to New England. Meanwhile the latter shed sent many of its charges, including this one, away on a northwards cascade to either Doncaster or Grantham. No.60858 ended up at the former shed but spent most of its time there in storage. By October it was time to take account and the V2 was condemned on the 6th - just twenty-four years old. Still it was nice to have a bit of green on Retford shed during those years to rundown. *BLP - E974*

Reflected in the tranquil waters of the River Idle, A4 No.60022 MALLARD heads south with an evening express in early September 1959. Looking at the amount of coal still in the tender, the Pacific has not come far and was probably put on this train at Doncaster which would possibly make it as being ex Hull (Paragon). The stock does not give any clues and Keith's notes are somewhat sketchy too. Perhaps he was just enjoying the view and the ambience of the whole scene which, you must admit, is rather nice on film. It is a pity the sounds of birdsong before and after the passing train, along with the smell of wild flowers which make for a memorable late summer evening cannot be reproduced as well. Until technology comes up with the goods, we will just have to make do with scenes like this for now although the Argo Transacord records (remember them? - EAF 33 in mono features the LNER Pacifics) sometimes feature a rural 'before and after' lineside recording. *BLP-E1719*

The *YORKSHIRE PULLMAN* was something of a late starter from Leeds (Central), leaving around mid-morning, although the times varied slightly from one year to the next. By the time it came through Retford it was past midday with the onboard clientele dining at their seats in sumptuous Pullman style - what a way to travel. It was essentially a train for businessmen where the supplements, on top of the first or second class fares, kept the train exclusive to those who could afford to travel aboard. Trainspotters and enthusiasts just marvelled at the opulence of the interiors of such luxury trains hoping that one day they too would be able to travel within the confines of the Pullman experience. Alas, those days are long gone and Pullman trains on the ECML or indeed any other part of the old BR system are no more. At the head of this Up service, passing through Ordsall in May 1960, is Copley Hill A1 No.60118 ARCHIBALD STURROCK. *BLP - E1716* 51

It would be impossible to capture this view today! Yes we do have a brand new Peppercorn A1 within our midst and the coaching stock would not be too hard to marshall, the wiring on the ECML could cause a problem but the main reason for the aforementioned statement is because the field and riverbank on which Keith Pirt was standing taking this June 1959 picture, has been built over. Anyway, note the wet smoke reflected in the water at the bend of the Idle. The engine is A1 No.60118 again, on a Leeds-King's Cross express. Note the signals, box and station buildings in the left distance showing the original borders between man and nature in this part of the world. Is this a flood plain? Why did the railway companies go to the expense of building their iron roads well above the original ground level? BLP - E1699

'...a structure carrying a road or railway over a valley...' is how the dictionary describes a viaduct. No mention of how many arches if any, so, the three-arch Gamston viaduct obviously qualifies for the title even though it is one of the less spectacular structures on the British Railways system. V2 No.60966 is crossing the viaduct, situated a couple of miles south of Retford, in April 1960 with a Down empty fish train bound for Hull. Just seventeen years old, this New England based 2-6-2 is in a deplorable external condition, more reminiscent of a much neglected WD 2-8-0 than a first-line mixed traffic locomotive. New England depot (was there a competition going on between 34E and 52A?) was not renowned for keeping its charges in a reasonably clean condition but this one must qualify for one of their dirtiest. However, four months after this scene was captured it entered the works at Darlington for a much needed General overhaul and came out looking somewhat smarter than this. *BLP - E1690*

This was the view from the north bank of the Idle, looking south from an elevated perch level with the main line. With all the drama that they mustered, A4 No.60001 SIR RONALD MATTHEWS, runs onto the bridge with a heavy northbound express in September 1959, the chime whistle having been sounded for the benefit of Keith. There are no prizes for guessing which depot this 'Streak' belonged to but to give you a clue, No.60001 worked as much to Edinburgh as it did to the south end of the ECML or at least the great changeover point at Grantham. A lot of people presume that the cleaning of ECML Pacifics started to fall off about the beginning of 1962 but this picture tells a different story - it was a Gateshead engine. Although the external condition of the 52A Pacific left a lot to be desired, it did not affect the engine's ability to haul these trains within the parameters of the working timetable. On the right of the picture can be seen part of Ordsall lake, a body of water which separated the railway from the meandering River Idle as it flowed through the district. Just south of the Down side signal post, a subway which linked the Thrumpton and Ordsall areas of Retford burrows under the main line, the parapet walls are just visible from this angle. Note the overflow channel alongside the railway acting as flood defences. We do not normally get this aspect of the bridge from Keith so it makes a nice change and reveals the signal wires strung across the outside of the bridge parapet, note the pulley wheels fixed to the timber bracket on the left. *BLP - E1687*

Heading an Up Newcastle express, double chimney A3 No.60108 GAY CRUSADER (I wonder how many people have taken up handbags at dawn to purchase that nameplate????) crosses the River Idle bridge south of the town during a late May evening in 1960. The King's Cross based Pacific had been given a double chimney during a 'General' in May 1959, however, like the rest of the class so treated, and that was all of them eventually, the double chimney and blastpipe had a softer blast which did not properly clear the smoke at speed. The solution to this visibility problem was to fit smoke deflectors which, in the case of the A3s, except for No.60097, saw the trough type German deflectors fitted during 1960 and 1961 to the class. From this more usual KRP stance at the Idle bridge, we can see the aforementioned wooden bracket and signal wires situated just where the tender is connected to the engine. BLP - E1688

Keith Pirt certainly knew his way around the waters of Retford and in this afternoon shot taken during March 1959, we are looking at a northbound express approaching Retford station and seen from across the Ordsall lake. The train engine is Thompson A2/3 No.60513 DANTE which, even at this distance does not look quite right at the front end. Nevertheless, the design idiosyncrasy of the locomotive does not detract from an otherwise pleasing view of what might have been an early spring in Nottinghamshire. *BLP - E1673*

Just a few hundred yards south of the flat crossing at Retford, V2 No.60867 gets into its stride with an Up, late afternoon, express in August 1958. The junction signals and the outline of the former Great Central main line are visible in the right background, atop their embankment, whilst in the left background can be seen the water softener and water tower at the former great Northern engine shed which backed onto the GC main albeit with a small cattle market in between the two. In the Down direction the ECML is quiet for the time being, according to the signals anyway. The lay-by siding, the sleepers of which are still of the creosote impregnated timber type contrast with the concrete sleepers and flat bottom rail of the main line tracks. Note however that short rail lengths were still being used on the Up and Down lines - continuously welded rail had still to make a big impact of BR - the reassuring clickerty-click of the carriage wheels had a hypnotic effect for many rail travellers in those days (not including enthusiasts of course). *BLP - E1674*

SWITCH

Not all of the east to west passenger services over the former GC line stopped at Retford. This express which originated in the Great Eastern area was certainly not booked to stop as it glides over the flat crossing in October 1958 with Colchester based B1 No.61363 in charge, complete with GE area disc code. This working may have been the Harwich-Liverpool (Central) boat train [*NORTH COUNTRY CONTINENTAL*] because the timing, according to the sun and shadows is about midday or shortly afterwards when this service was due through Retford. but it was unusual to have a Thompson B1 working the trains when Gresley B17s were still the preferred choice. Perhaps the intended B17 was a failure and the B1 stepped in with impeccable timing. The condition of the engine suggests a visit to main works has recently taken place and indeed that was the case because the 4-6-0 left the works at Stratford on 3rd October after a five-week long General overhaul which saw the bogie springs modified. Although based for the whole of its life in former GER territory, this engine made its final journey over this crossing heading westward to Lancashire and the Central Wagon Co.scrapyard at Wigan in 1963. Note the two school boys on the stilted concrete platform, which curved round from the station's No.1 platform, is it lunch time or half-term? Hopefully, they were not too disappointed to see the B1 which, being based where it was, would have been a rare bird in Retford anyway. BLP - E1671

Yet another view of the flat crossing with O2 No.63926 taking advantage of a lull in the north-south traffic pattern to get across with its eastbound mineral train in August 1958. Note the Down main line loop had been busy on this date with the rails looking very shiny. *BLP - E1668*

As seen from the Great North Road - the eastern end of Thrumpton shed yard in October 1961 with LNER built Gresley O2 No.63946 prominent at the buffer stops. The overhead wires feeding current to the electrically operated turntable can just be made out hanging down from their post to the central collection gantry on the turntable, the position of which can be approximated behind the wagons situated to the right of the locomotives. No.63946 had not long since arrived at Retford after an eight year stint at Grantham. Just beyond the chimney of the O2 we can see the tender top of an unidentified O4. Note the red lead paint scheme afforded by Gorton to the parts the public did not usually see. Most other workshops took the black paint over the water filler and into the coal bunker. *BLP - E1216*

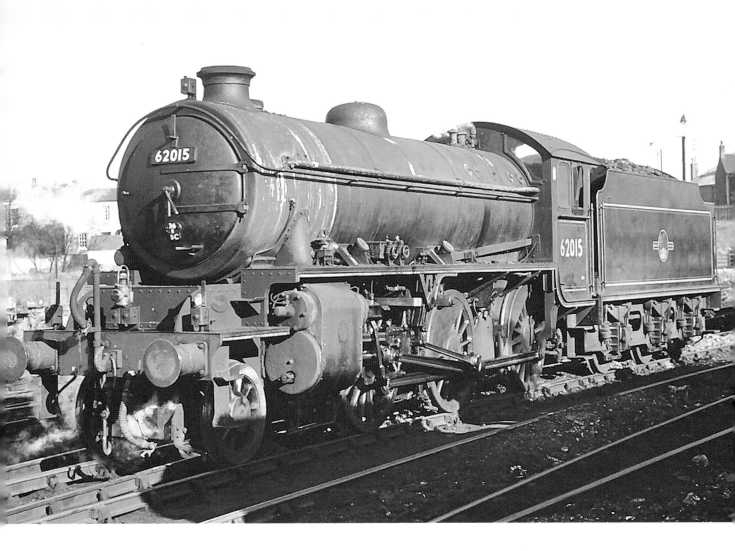

The north-east corner of Thrumpton engine shed yard in November 1962 with the turntable just visible behind the tender of resident K1 No.62015. Also visible, to the left, is one of the then growing number of 350 h.p. 0-6-0 diesel-electric shunting locomotives which were taking over much of the work in the local yards. The yard work did not affect the engines allocated to this ex GC shed, all of their charges were involved in moving coal along the main lines from pit to destination and then returning with the empties. The former GN shed took care of the shunting locomotives and any necessary passenger and parcels jobs. Both sheds of course came under the same code 36E and the same foreman. The historic layout at Retford gave the GC shed the advantage of getting engines off to the collieries without any shunting or doubling back to access the east-west main line. Being where it was situated alongside the station, the GN depot was ideal for supplying the motive power for any passenger trains and yard shunting. Getting engines onto the Sheffield line from there involved a bit of shunting, toing and froing. *BLP - E1605*

Retford K1 No.62054 rounds the platform (No.1) curve from the GN main to the GC main at Retford in October 1962 with a Lincoln line coal train. The curved platform is now gone as are the signals in the background. *BLP - E1653*

How's that for a smoke affect? A3 No.60046 DIAMOND JUBILEE heads an Up express through the cutting south of the old A1 road bridge. The Down signal is also hidden by the smoke. *BLP - E1664*

Returning to Gamston, we now have the view from the other side of the track as A4 No.60007 SIR NIGEL GRESLEY passes the Gamston Home Up bracket signal in June 1961 under a rather weak sun. *BLP - E1661*

O2 No.63926 had been a resident of Retford since transferring from Doncaster on 3rd February 1952 and in this August 1961 view over the ashpits outside the Thrumpton shed, it is looking a little jaded but appearances can be deceiving and mechanically it was sound. Its GNR style Class B tender was the last of seven which the engine had been coupled to since coming into traffic in June 1921. This particular tender, T5098, had been with the engine since February 1947 and would go with it to Bulwell Forest Wagon Works (W.Rigley) in Nottingham when the pair were sold for scrap in late 1963. But that was some time off yet and another two years of hard work still lay ahead of the 2-8-0. The side window cab had been fitted in October 1940 when it was allocated to New England, where it spent its first twenty-two years. Over the years from August 1951, when the first O2s (Nos.63970, 63972, 63982) were allocated to Retford, no less than forty-two members of the class have been 'on the books'. Besides the original GN engines, all of the LNER variants have also been shedded. All but six of the forty-two were withdrawn at Retford and many spent ten years or more working from the depot. Doncaster shed had given Retford most of its O2s but other depots had also given with both Grantham and Mexborough sending eight each, whilst Frodingham sent three, No.63937 in October 1953 and Nos.63945 and 63961 in January 1954. *BLP - E1659*

What went on at 34A which saw most of their 'big engines' clean whilst at other sheds the external condition of the Pacific engines ranged from dirty to downright filthy? This is V2 No.60862 with the Up Scotch Goods (the first vehicle was a container flat which is not visible) crossing the Idle bridge at Ordsall in October 1962, a year after the 2-6-2s last repaint! The engine had its original monobloc cylinders replaced by separate cylinders in February 1957. Two years later a complete AWS (Automatic Warning System) was put on whilst in September 1961 a double chimney and Kylchap blastpipe were fitted. A lot of investment in a short time but to what end because in April 1963 the V2 transferred to New England and immediate storage, only to be condemned in the following June. *BLP - E1654*

Heading for home, King's Cross (which other shed could it have been?) V2 No.60983 with *THE SCARBOROUGH FLYER* at Ordsall in June 1960. This train has its origins back in 1880 when the GNR had a through service from King's Cross to both Scarborough and Whitby. The LNER were the first to name the train and in 1924 christened it *SCARBOROUGH FLIER* but no headboards were introduced until 1932. Throughout the LNER period up to 1939, when the Second World War intervened, the train was run non-stop to York and was hauled as far as that place by a Doncaster Pacific. When the service was resumed in 1950 a two-line headboard was used from the start but it was a revised version of the LNER board with THE preceding and above the title; FLIER was changed to FLYER. In 1952 the standard three-line headboard, as seen here, was introduced and carried until the train was dropped at the end of the 1962 summer timetable. The BR train did not really deserve the FLYER suffix as it took nearly five hours for both the Up and Down trains to reach their destinations; the pre-war timings were four hours and seven minutes including an engine change at York and the detaching of the Whitby portion. No.60983 would have coupled onto this train at York where a B1 would have brought the train from the coast at a leisurely pace. By some quirk of fate which saved embarrassment all round, the headboard was not carried by the engine working the York-Scarborough section of the journey. Note the diesel multiple unit in the background approaching the flat crossing with a Lincoln-Sheffield service. BLP - E1628

Peppercorn A1 No.60157 GREAT EASTERN passes the 138 milepost at Ordsall with a Newcastle-King's Cross express in February 1960. Note the exposed pipe at the front of the boiler behind the smoke deflector. Now based at Doncaster (it never was allocated to 52A or 34E), the Pacific is just a few weeks away from entering Doncaster Plant for what would be its penultimate General overhaul. *BLP - E1627*

WD 2-8-0 No.90662 heads a real miscellany of empty hopper wagons over the ECML flat crossing in October 1963. Note the cattle dock platform on the left which served the local cattle market situated at the rear of the Great Northern engine shed. By now the newly resident Austerities had taken over such work as this from the withdrawn O2s. At this time no less than twenty-one of the former Ministry of Supply 2-8-0s were allocated to Retford but No.90662 was not amongst their number and never would be; it was allocated to Immingham until condemned on Sunday 29th August 1965. *BLP - C3*

Another of the original Great Central Railway 8Ks, as BR No.63586 (note the small numerals on the cab side), in the siding alongside the south wall of Thrumpton shed in March 1962. Although it attended Gorton works once more before that place closed in 1963, the 2-8-0 only went for a Casual Light repair which lasted from 26th November 1962 to 11th January 1963 but by then the O4 would have moved from Retford shed anyway to Frodingham in September 1962, replaced by an O2 from Doncaster. This engine lasted until October 1965 but was then sold to a scrap merchant in Killamarsh. Its final journey would bring it past Thrumpton engine shed or to be more precise the site of the establishment because by then it would have been demolished as part of the new works affecting the dive-under scheme. In this view of the shed wall we can see the different bricks with the original 1849 wall reaching as far as the window openings whilst above is the new wall built to cater for the roof erected by BR. *BLP - E1306*

No.60103, looking rather filthy for a 34A Pacific, halts at Retford with an Up afternoon express in April 1959. *BLP - E30*

To finish off in grand style and to remind those who experienced the cold winter of 1962-63, we have A3 No.60070 GLADIATEUR heading south with a parcels train at Markham Moor in November 1962. The white woolly exhaust virtually completes a somewhat Christmas card type scene except that there is no snow on the ground - yet. *BLP - E322*